GETTING
THE
THIRD DEGREE

The Laurie Cunningham story

BY DOUGIE BLAXLAND

Published by Playdead Press 2019

© Dougie Blaxland 2019

Dougie Blaxland has asserted his rights under the
Copyright, Design and Patents Act, 1988, to be
identified as the author of this work.

A CIP catalogue record for this book is available from
the British Library.

ISBN 978-1-910067-84-0

Playdead Press
www.playdeadpress.com

Getting The Third Degree was first performed at the Wardrobe Theatre, Bristol, on 22nd October 2019 with the following cast:

ACTOR ONE:	**Sabrina Laurison**
ACTOR TWO:	**Emile Clarke**
ACTOR THREE:	**Zara Gabbidon**

Featuring the voices of:
Rhodene Cunningham, Garth Crooks and David Lammy.

Writer:	**Dougie Blaxland**
Directors:	**Moira Hunt & Shane Morgan**
Designed by:	**RoughHouse Theatre**
Commissioned by:	**Kick It Out**
Produced by:	**Live Wire Theatre & RoughHouse Theatre**

The company wish to thank:

Kick It Out, Colin Blumenau and The Production Exchange, Garth Crooks, David Lammy, Rhodene Cunningham, Dermot Kavanagh (*Different Class: The Story of Laurie Cunningham* available at www.unbound.com), Carole Banwell and Bath City FC, David Langley and Prior Park College, Ian McGlynn and the Rondo Theatre, Tobacco Factory Theatres Bristol, Joe Kennedy and Nimko Ali (*What We're Told Not To Talk About* available at www.penguin.co.uk)

Please note: This is the final draft and rehearsal ready script. Changes may have been made between the time of going to press and opening night.

'In our life there is a single colour which provides the meaning of life and art…
It is the colour of love.'

Marc Chagall

"He inspired a whole generation of young black kids to believe that they too could overcome prejudice and bigotry to fulfil their potential..."

I know that I'm speaking for everyone in the Cunningham family when I say that not a day goes by when we don't all think about Laurie and remember him with the deep love and affection that he radiated when he was still with us.

I was only a young girl when he was taken so tragically from us on 15th July 1989 but the impact that he had on me and everyone close to him has never diminished. Although quietly spoken and gentle there was something magical in his nature that was deeply fascinating. Indeed, without ever being demonstrative or 'showy', people were instinctively drawn by his magnetic charisma.

He is, of course, remembered most widely today as a footballer who combined blistering pace with superb ball control and dazzling footwork to match. As the first black player to play for the mighty Real Madrid and only the second to win a full England cap he will always have a place in sporting history but his legacy goes way beyond that. The artistry and skill that he brought onto the football field not only forced comparisons with the great Pele but also brought what was a unique accolade for a Real Madrid player: a standing ovation from the Barcelona crowd at the Nou Camp having ripped the home team apart.

What we are proudest of as a family, however, is the undeniable fact that together with his dear friends Cyrille Regis and Brendan Batson he inspired a whole generation of young black kids to believe that they too could overcome prejudice and bigotry to fulfil their potential in whatever field they chose.

The magical spirit of my wonderful uncle was such that he defied any stereotypes or categorisation. He was a man of super cool style and elegance who also wrote poetry, enjoyed painting and engaging in discussions on profound philosophical issues. He was also a brilliant freestyle dancer who combined the explosive energy of an athlete with the grace of ballet winning numerous competitions and cash prizes at the coolest clubs in town.

It is a huge testament to my uncle that thirty years on from his death he is still remembered and celebrated. In recent years, as a family, we have witnessed the unveiling of plaques and statues, attended commemorative events and assisted with research for books and documentary programmes about his life. We are now really excited that he will be brought back to life on stage, if only for 90 minutes each night during the tour of *Getting The Third Degree*.

Above all though, the Cunningham family remembers Laurie as our son, brother, uncle, husband and father. He was the magic dust of our lives that made us feel special and everything seem possible.

Rhodene Cunningham

"He brought hope and inspiration to a whole generation of young black footballers."

I was a young starry eyed professional with Stoke City when Laurie Cunningham exploded onto the scene. I had only played a handful of games in the first division meanwhile Laurie was tearing defences to shreds during the 1978/79 season. West Bromwich Albion were the team to watch in the Midlands at that time.

In the pioneering days of the late 1970's there were only a handful of black footballers in the professional game and I would follow all their careers with great interest but none of them captured my imagination like Laurie.

West Brom was only a few miles down the M6 from Stoke and I made it my business to see for myself if this kid was as good as everyone said he was.

I made the journey to The Hawthorns to watch him play against Valencia in the UEFA Cup 3rd round second leg and Laurie was magical. It wasn't just his blistering turn of pace that set him apart from the rest of the players on the field; he was so smooth, he seemed to 'dance' past defenders.

I met Laurie much later through Cyrille Regis but I never told him the impact he had on me. Indeed, Laurie Cunningham was my inspiration – a role model.

Laurie played football with the swagger of Ian Wright, the ability of John Barnes the style and panache of Thierry Henry. There was nothing he couldn't do. He brought excitement, ingenuity, fashion and flair to a game that was often dull and at times predictable. However, far more importantly than that, he brought hope and inspiration to a whole generation of young black footballers.

Garth Crooks

"Crossing over and having conversations are how you change hearts and minds."

Racism is real and with the growth of populism it's now being normalised because we have lost the ability to counter it with facts. All hate is based in fear and racism is no different. I cannot count the number of times someone has said something racist and then followed it with, "but not you Nimko. You are not like them". I am not sure which 'them' they are speaking of because when it comes to hating the other, I am many of those who are being vilified. I am black yes, but I am also African and I am also from a refugee background and yes, I am Muslim. When I hear the line, "but not you Nimko", I always reply, "but you mean my mum, sister and a million people I know and love". That stops them and in the moment of silence I take the time to explain how people like me are also racist and say horrid things about white people or non-Muslims. When I correct them, I say the same thing to white racists I meet in suits or t-shirts, you are entitled to like or date who you want. But the truth is you have been raised to fear difference because if you took a second and got to know the people you hate, you will find they are just like you. And you assume that everyone is here to take something from you but in reality, immigration has given more to the UK than it's taken away. Crossing over and having conversations are how you change hearts and minds. People will always say things we find offensive but it's up to us if we take offence or not. I choose not to be offended but to use moments for open dialogue which is not something you owe people but it is something that if you have the privilege and platform, you should take advantage of.

Nimko Ali

Co-founder of The Five Foundation
Author of *What We're Told Not To Talk About (But We're Going To Anyway)*
www.penguin.co.uk

The Play opens with the 3 Actors as a group singing 'When Will I see You Again' by The Three Degrees (1973)

ALL: *(singing)* Hoo-oo ha-a ha-a hoo-oo
           Precious moments
           When will I see you again
           When will we share precious moments
           Will I have to wait forever
           Will I have to suffer
           And cry the whole night through?
           When will I see you again
           When will our hearts beat together?
           Are we in love or just friends?
           Is this my beginning
           Or is this the end?
           When will I see you again?
           When will I see you again?
           When will I see you again?

(There is an abrupt end to the music and the 3 Actors become fans on the terraces at a West Bromwich Albion match)

ALL: *(singing the WBA anthem)* Albion, Albion, Albion,
           Albion, Albion, Albion,
           Albion, Albion, Albion,
           Albion!
           Aaalllbbbiooon! *(Repeat)*

(The 3 Actors combine the roles of commentators and Laurie Cunningham)

ACTOR 1:   *(commentating as Actors 2 & 3 both and enact the event as Laurie Cunningham)* And that's a beautiful pass to Cunningham and if he keeps his head he'll score - oh yes - into bottom right hand corner - pure perfection!

ACTOR 2: *(commentating as Actors 1 & 3 both and enact the event as Laurie Cunningham)* Cunningham's got to get past Carete – and he does – just as if he's not there – and - my word – what a shot – and it's there – he's scored – Albion take the lead.

ACTOR 3: *(commentating as Actors 1 & 2 both and enact the event as Laurie Cunningham)* And here comes Cunningham again – past Coppell – past McCreary – such speed – such grace - such ease – and – and – *(beat)* – what a goal – what - a – goal!

ALL: *(chanting as the WBA crowd)*

(Clap, clap, clap, clap, clap),

Laurie

(Clap, clap, clap, clap, clap),

Laurie

(Clap, clap, clap, clap, clap),

Laurie

(The Actors address the audience directly)

ACTOR 1: But long before they chanted his name

From the Brummie Road end in games he played at the Hawthorns: -

ACTOR 2: And before Real Madrid crowds

10

Hailed the 'Black Pearl' at the Bernabeu.

ALL: *(chanting as the Real Madrid crowd)* La Perla Negra *(clap, clap, clap)*

La Perla Negra *(clap, clap, clap)*

ACTOR 3: And long before his dazzling feet

Forced full backs into retreat –

ACTOR 2: Left them mesmerised.

ACTOR 1: Entranced.

ACTOR 3: As he glided.

ACTOR 2: Floated.

ACTOR 1: Danced his way goalwards.

ACTOR 3: Long long before this -

ACTOR 2: We remember a freezing Rotherham day in December 1930

(The 3 Actors stand as if at a graveside during a funeral. They become The Priest (Actor 1), Gravedigger (Actor 2) and Undertaker (Actor 3) and also give commentary on the events).

ACTOR 3: A gravedigger –

ACTOR 1: An undertaker –

ACTOR 2: Reluctant parish priest -

ACTOR 3: Stand at the grave of a man deceased and forgotten –

ACTOR 1: *(as the priest)* Almighty God – into your hands we commend your son – your son – *(he cannot remember the name of the deceased)*

ACTOR 3: *(prompting the priest)* Arthur Bourton –

ACTOR 2: *(correcting his colleague)* Wharton – Arthur Wharton – the goalkeeper –

(Actor 3 expresses his recognition of Arthur Wharton)

ACTOR 1: …in sure and certain hope…

ACTOR 2: Professional debut Rotherham Town 1889.

ACTOR 1: …certain hope of resurrection…

ACTOR 3: Rotherham Town then Sheffield United.

ACTOR 1: …resurrection to eternal life

ACTOR 2: Stockport County & Stalybridge Rovers.

ACTOR 1: …eternal life through Jesus Christ our Lord…

ACTOR 3: Not to forget Preston North End.

ACTOR 1: …through Jesus Christ our Lord - Amen. *(Beat)* This body we commit to the ground –

ACTOR 2: *(direct to the audience)* A pauper's plot –

ACTOR 3: *(direct to the audience)* A barely distinguishable mound of earth –

ACTOR 1: *(he says the first word in concert with Actor 2)* Earth to earth…

ACTOR 2:   *(direct to the audience)* A black man in the white man's game.

ACTOR 1:   Ashes to ashes dust to dust.

ACTOR 3:   *(direct to the audience)* Departing life without fortune or fame or representation.

ACTOR 1:   Blessed are the dead who die in the Lord.

Yes, says the Spirit, they will rest from their labors

For their deeds follow them.

ACTOR 2:   *(direct to the audience)* Not his – not Arthur Wharton's deeds.

ACTOR 3:   Which could have seen - could have been the seeds of change.

(All three in unison act out a choreographed illustration of his goalkeeping skills as Arthur Wharton)

ACTOR 2:   For all his heart in hurling black body groundwards to compete with the leather booted feet of marauding centre forwards -

ACTOR 1:   For all those arch backed limbo lithe dives –

ACTOR 3:   Those full stretch fingertip saves –

ACTOR 1:   For all that - little survives.

ACTOR 2:   No headstone however plain.

ACTOR 1:   No date of birth –

ACTOR 3: No record of his name –

ACTOR 2: No mark or sign that he had kith or kin –

ACTOR 1: Not that he was written out 'cos he was never written in.

ACTOR 3: And so, we raise him up anew.

(They raise an imaginary coffin as pallbearers and walk to a slow march)

ACTOR 2: We say farewell.

ACTOR 1: We bid adieu now as befits a pioneer -

ACTOR 3: We say that name again here and now -

ALL: Arthur Wharton

ACTOR 3: African born –

ACTOR 2: Dying forlorn of mourners –

ACTOR 1: The first black man in the white man's game –

ACTOR 3: Whose career like his coffin lay buried deep in time with few following behind.

ACTOR 2: But two.

ACTOR 1: Two men of colour who in Arthur Wharton's lifetime went so far as to brave football's colour bar.

(They salute Walter Tull's name as it if reading a remembrance roll-call)

ACTOR 2: So, we sing out their names -

ACTOR 1:   Walter Tull.

ACTOR 1:   Grandson of slaves from Barbados.

(Actor 1 stands in the traditional pose of Walter Tull as a footballer)

ACTOR 3:   Wing half for Spurs.

ACTOR 2:   Then Northampton Town:

ACTOR 2:   Before heeding Kitchener's rallying sound:

(They enact the poster of Lord Kitchener pointing)

ALL: 'Your Country Needs You!'

(The 3 Actors now become military personnel at a WW1 recruitment centre – Music – WW1 Song Over There)

ACTOR 2:   If you want to enlist just join the queue.

ACTOR 3:   Sign here my lad.

ACTOR 2:   *(patronising)* A cross will do just as well my son.

ACTOR 1:   I can write my own name thank you very much!

ACTOR 3:   *(with heavy sarcasm)* Hear that George! We've got Officer material!

ACTOR 1:   And why not?

ACTOR 2:   *(continuing the sarcasm)* Why not! Did you hear him John! Why not! That's a laugh!

ACTOR 3:   Never looked in the mirror then son?

(Actor 2 and 3 laugh uproariously)

15

ACTOR 1:   *(direct to the audience)* Promoted to Sergeant before too long

ACTOR 2:   He was commissioned an officer after The Somme –

ACTOR 3:   And led his men one fine Spring day

In a frontal attack near to Pas De Calais in Northern France.

(Actor 1 is Walter Tull and Actors 2 and 3 are members of his platoon)

ACTOR 1:   Wait for my whistle - do you hear me - wait -

Heads down, stay low, keep out of sight

On the whistle's blast - it's up and over -

I'll be with you - so 'here's to fate' -

'Cos bullets don't discriminate between rank or race.

And make it fast - just run like hell -

(Actor 1 blows the whistle and they all enacts getting out of a trench and running across No Man's Land before Actor 1 falls at the sound of gunfire)

ACTOR 2:   And the exact spot where Walter Tull fell isn't known – not the exact spot.

ACTOR 3:   And all that his mother ever got -

(Actor 2 becomes a postman knocking at the Mrs Tull's door)

ACTOR 2:   Mrs Tull?

ACTOR 3:   Yes.

ACTOR 2:   Telegram.

(Actor 2 hands Actor 3 a telegram which is then opened as Actor 1 rises)

ACTOR 1:   *(speaking the words in the telegram)* 'Regret – stop – Lieutenant Walter Tull – stop – killed in action – stop – March 25th 1918 – stop.

(Beat)

ACTOR 2:   You could die for your country – black – white – all the same – but football – that was the white man's game.

(The 3 Actors form a guard of honour to salute Jack Leslie's name)

ACTOR 1:   And so, we sing out Jack Leslie's name.

ACTOR 2:   Jack Leslie – born of Jamaican descent.

(Actor 2 stands in the traditional pose of Jack Leslie as a footballer)

ACTOR 3:   Joined Plymouth Argyle intent on making his way in the game. 1921 to 1934 *(Actor 2 enacts goal scoring routine)*

ACTOR 1:   A centre forward he scored goals galore.

ACTOR 3:   400 or more – so many in fact – that international recognition came his way.

17

ACTOR 1: Letter dated March 14th 1928

ACTOR 2: *(still as Jack Leslie)* 'Dear Mr Leslie – we wish to extend an invitation for you to play for England...'

ACTOR 1: A few days later – a telegram:

ACTOR 2: *(still as Jack Leslie)* 'With regret – we write to inform - our invitation has been withdrawn.'

ACTOR 3: Can somebody please explain!

(They all become England selectors)

ACTOR 2: We selected Leslie on reputation -

ACTOR 1: No-one here at The FA has actually seen him play.

ACTOR 3: Plymouth is two hundred and fifty miles away from London.

ACTOR 2: A simple mistake.

ACTOR 1: Had we known his complexion -

ACTOR 2: We're talking about the colour of his face.

ACTOR 1: Exactly so.

ACTOR 3: We wouldn't have picked him in the first place.

ACTOR 2: It's not as if he's really British -

ACTOR 1: *(whispering the embarrassing correction)* Actually – he was born in Canning Town.

ACTOR 3: Yes, but not British in the true sense of the word.

(They briefly revert to being themselves)

ACTOR 1:   But things move on.

ACTOR 2:   1948 – the 13th of May.

ACTOR 3:   Kingston Jamaica.

(They become a family in Jamaica in May 1948 – Music – Jamaica Farewell – Harry Belafonte)

ACTOR 1:   Hey, listen here to what it says in The Gleaner:

ACTOR 2:   What's it says?

ACTOR 1:   *(He reads a Jamaican newspaper advertisement from June 1948)* 'Under the terms of British Nationality Act' –

ACTOR 3:   Passed earlier this year.

ACTOR 2:   Is that a fact?

ACTOR 1:   *(continuing to read)* Citizens of former British Colonies – may be entitled to Citizenship of The British Empire – and if you are hardworking –

ACTOR 3:   I would be if I could get a job –

ACTOR 1:   *(continuing to read)* clean living and in need of employment –

ACTOR 2:   That's us –

ACTOR 1:   *(continuing to read)* – you can apply for passage on The Empire Windrush –

ACTOR 3:   How can we possibly afford that!

ACTOR 1: *(continuing to read)* 'Subsidised fares are available'.

ACTOR 2: When do we go?

ACTOR 3: *(continuing to read)* – departing for London on 17th June. For more information contact The British Colonial Office at 28 Trafalgar Rd Kingston Jamaica.'

(The Actors now become arrivals at Tilbury London as the actual recording from Pathe News is heard)

Recording of the Voice from The Pathe Newsreel:
Arrivals at Tilbury – The Empire Windrush brings to Britain 500 Jamaicans - many ex-servicemen who know England they served this country well. In Jamaica they couldn't find work. Discouraged but full of hope they sailed for Britain. Citizens of the British Empire coming to the Mother Country with good intent. Courted by public opinion the Colonial Office gives them a more cordial reception than was at first envisaged. Many are to be found jobs.

(The Actors briefly become Windrush arrivals reading advertisements for jobs)

ACTOR 1: *(as if reading a newspaper advertisement)* 'Wanted – Warehouse Caretaker – Central London' –

ACTOR 2: *(completing the reading of the advertisement)* – 'No blacks need apply'.

ACTOR 3:   *(as if reading a newspaper advertisement)* 'Wanted – shop assistant for leading Birmingham store – training given' –

ACTOR 1:   *(completing the reading of the advertisement)* – 'Whites only'.

ACTOR 2:   *(as if reading a newspaper advertisement)* Rooms available for rent – East Manchester –

ACTOR 3:   'No Irish' –

ACTOR 1:   'No dogs' –

ACTOR 2:   'No Blacks'.

(They revert to being themselves)

ACTOR 2:   But our grandmas, grandads, ma's and pa's - they brave the discrimination.

ACTOR 3:   More ships sail – more planes come –

ACTOR 1:   Bringing the Windrush generation to a Great British welcome.

(The Actors become Mavis Cunningham and Coldly Efficient Interviewers at The Islington Labour Exchange)

ACTOR 1:   *(as if barking an instruction)* Name.

ACTOR 2:   Mavis

ACTOR 1:   *(snapping an emphatic correction)* Full name.

ACTOR 2:   Mavis Cunningham.

ACTOR 3:   Address.

ACTOR 2: 3 Brookside Place North London.

ACTOR 3: Arrival date.

ACTOR 2: Last week.

ACTOR 1: Exact date.

ACTOR 2: Saturday the 3rd December 1955.

ACTOR 3: Husband's name.

ACTOR 2: Elias Cunningham.

ACTOR 1: Occupation.

ACTOR 2: He's a jockey. *(Beat)* He's very good – very successful.

ACTOR 3: Why isn't he with you?

ACTOR 2: Elias is still in Jamaica with our little boy, Keith.

ACTOR 1: You mean to say that you left your child to come to England?

ACTOR 2: We could only afford the one ticket.

ACTOR 3: I see.

ACTOR 1: And what kind of work are you looking for?

ACTOR 2: I'll do anything – anything at all.

ACTOR 3: We have a vacancy at Bristol Laundry off the Holloway Road.

ACTOR 1: And another at the The Eagle Pencil factory in Tottenham.

ACTOR 2: Either would be fine.

ACTOR 3: Very well but before I send your details out to any potential employers one final question *(Beat)* When is the baby actually due?

(The Actors revert to become themselves)

ACTOR 1: 1956 – March the 8th.

ACTOR 2: At Whittington Hospital London they celebrate the birth.

(The Actors become 2 Midwives and Mavis Cunningham)

ACTOR 3: *(lifting up an imaginary baby and passing him to Actor 1)* It's a boy Mrs Cunningham.

ACTOR 1: *(putting the baby in imaginary scales)* Seven pounds four ounces!

ACTOR 3: And do you have a name for the baby yet Mrs Cunningham.

ACTOR 2: I think Lawrence is a nice name.

ACTOR 1: Lawrence.

ACTOR 2: Lawrence Paul Cunningham.

ACTOR 3: It certainly has a ring to it.

ACTOR 1: *(addressing the imaginary baby)* Nice to meet you Lawrence Paul Cunningham I wonder what you'll do with your life.

(The Actors become working men in a pub)

ACTOR 2:   Have you read this morning's paper?

ACTOR 1:   Why what's it say?

ACTOR 2:   *(repeating the question with increasing emphasis)* What's it say? What's it say?

ACTOR 3:   Well – what does it say?

ACTOR 2:   Breeding!

ACTOR 1:   Who's breeding what?

ACTOR 2:   They are – them – 'blackies' – breeding more 'blackies –

ACTOR 3:   Taking over – that's what's happening…

ACTOR 1:   Half a million – that's what they reckon – that's how many's come – since they opened the floodgates.

ACTOR 2:   And now there's all this breeding.

ACTOR 3:   Won't know ourselves in a few years.

ACTOR 1:   Someone should say something – speak out – before it's too late.

(The 3 Actors become Enoch Powell and members of his audience – Music – I Heard it Through The Grapevine – Marvin Gaye – 1968)

ACTOR 3:   *(as Enoch Powell in a Conservative Party blue rosette)* A week or two ago I fell into conversation with a constituent, a middle-aged, quite

24

ordinary working man employed in one of our nationalised industries. After a sentence or two about the weather, he suddenly said: "If I had the money to go, I wouldn't stay in this country."

ACTOR 1: Nor would I.

ACTOR 2: Nor me – not the way things are going.

ACTOR 1: *(continuing as Enoch Powell)* I made some deprecatory reply to the effect that even this government wouldn't last forever; but he took no notice, and continued: "I have three children, all of them been through grammar school and two of them married now, with family. I shan't be satisfied till I have seen them all settled overseas. In this country in 15 or 20-years' time the black man will have the whip hand over the white man."

ACTOR 3: He certainly has a point.

ACTOR 2: Couldn't agree more – I mean – they come over – take our jobs.

ACTOR 3: And our women.

ACTOR 2: It's the thin end of the wedge.

ACTOR 3: It's why I go to the football mate – only place you don't see a black face.

ACTOR 2: And long may it stay like that – football I mean –

(The Music of the 1964 Dylan song 'The Times They Are a Changin' is played. Actor 1 switches from being Enoch Powell to being the Liberal Voice)

ACTOR 1: *(as the Liberal Voice)* But what about Brazil – I mean – you can't ignore the sheer thrill – the scintillating skill of Pele – he's the best – the very best. Our 'donkey plodders' don't begin to compete.

(The Actors revert to being themselves)

ACTOR 1: And along comes this boy with such dazzling feet—

ACTOR 2: In synchronised beat with body and soul -

(The sound of rhythmic beats begins and they move together in 'sync' in a dancing sequence speaking to the words in time to the beat of the music)

ACTOR 3: *(speaking in the rhythm of the musical beat)* Ska, 2 Tone, reggae, blues –

Are the rhythm of his lissom moves –

ACTOR 1: The gliding, quick step –

ACTOR 2: Heel turn, swerving –

ACTOR 3: Zig zag dashes, chasse, curving –

ACTOR 1: Free wheel, heel turn –

ACTOR 2: Hip hop, spin –

ACTOR 3: Like a will-of-the-wisp he whips up the wing –

ACTOR 1:   Past flailing defences –

ACTOR 2:   Elusive –

ACTOR 3:   Free –

ALL: Beyond mere words

ACTOR 1:   Beyond poetry's power to distil this moment –

ACTOR 2:   To hold it in time –

ACTOR 3:   So, fleeting of foot that before any rhyme comes to mind –

ALL: *(they blow in a synchronised movement into cupped hands and then open them to see what's there)*

Gone!

(The sound of rhythmic beats ends and the Actors revert to become a small choir singing the Nina Simone song 'Young Gifted and Black')

ALL: *(singing)*
To be young, gifted and black,
Oh, what a lovely precious dream
To be young, gifted and black,
Open your heart to what I mean.
In the whole world you know
There are billion boys and girls
Who are young gifted and black
And that's a fact.

(The actors become two Arsenal scouts and Bob Cottingham)

ACTOR 1: Well – if it ain't Bob Cottingham! Good to see you Bob?

ACTOR 2: Yes – good to see you Bob –

ACTOR 1: How's that Highgate boys' team of yours doing mate?

ACTOR 2: And what brings you to the Arsenal? Got any young talent to send our way?

ACTOR 1: We're always on the lookout for young talent at Arsenal

ACTOR 3: That's why I'm here.

ACTOR 2: *(back pedalling)* Not that we can guarantee to see every boy recommended.

ACTOR 3: I've come about young Laurie Cunningham.

ACTOR 1: We've had to let young Cunningham go – I'm afraid.

ACTOR 2: Sad day.

ACTOR 1: Always a sad day.

ACTOR 2: Never really got to know him – mind.

ACTOR 1: Kept himself to himself.

ACTOR 2: Hardly ever said a word.

ACTOR 3: That's 'cos he's shy.

ACTOR 2: Shy or not – he wasn't up to the mark I'm afraid.

ACTOR 1: Not the mark we set at the Arsenal.

ACTOR 3: I don't suppose you'd reconsider.

ACTOR 1: We gave him his chance Bob.

ACTOR 2: Every possible chance.

ACTOR 1: He was a regular in the Boys' Team.

ACTOR 2: Two years we gave him and you can't be fairer than that.

ACTOR 3: But every game he played – and I watched almost every one – every game – you stuck him out wide – totally isolated – bollocked every time he tried to move more central – and that's the way you play – through the centre – I mean – he hardly ever ever got the ball –

ACTOR 2: Every boy who comes to us has to learn to play our way.

ACTOR 1: The way we play the game in England.

(The Actors now become like a military unit on a parade ground going through a squad drill)

ACTOR 1: Well drilled.

ACTOR 2: High work rate.

ACTOR 3: Full discipline.

ACTOR 1: Conform to the system.

ACTOR 2: They have to fit in.

ACTOR 1: Whole hearted effort.

ACTOR 2:   Total dedication.

ACTOR 1:   No breaking ranks

ACTOR 3:   No insubordination.

(They revert to becoming two Arsenal scouts and Bob Cottingham)

ACTOR 1:   So, you see Bob – you go back and tell your boys at Highgate North Hill – we don't want none of that flashy football Cunningham goes in for.

ACTOR 2:   He's not the right material – not for us – not for English football.

ACTOR 3:   I think you're making a big mistake.

ACTOR 1:   I admire your intentions Bob – you know – giving the boy a fatherly helping hand and all that –

ACTOR 3:   It's got nothing to do with that – the boy's the best I've seen – and we've had some good ones at Highgate North Hill – we really have.

ACTOR 2:   We know that but Cunningham hasn't got what it takes – not as far as attitude goes, he hasn't.

ACTOR 1:   And that's what matters most – attitude.

ACTOR 2:   To be frank – it's what they all lack.

ACTOR 3:   They?

ACTOR 1:   Them – you know what I mean.

ACTOR 2:   Different culture.

ACTOR 1: Not their fault of course.

ACTOR 2: It's just the way they are.

ACTOR 3: What about Eusebio and Pele?

ACTOR 2: Of course, they're exceptions to every rule.

ACTOR 2: But in the main – you only have to watch them in training.

ACTOR 1: No stamina.

ACTOR 3: Laurie is the fittest boy who's ever played for me at Highgate North Hill.

ACTOR 2: He's all right in flashes.

ACTOR 3: And that's the word for him – 'flash'.

ACTOR 2: I mean – let's be honest – where the Cunningham boys concerned – and all of his kind in fact – apart from the obvious exceptions - with them – you know – his sort – it's all a question of temperament.

ACTOR 1: Exactly – they haven't got the temperament – not for the modern game – not for how we play in 1972.

(The Actors become Laurie Cunningham (Actor 2), Bob Cottingham (Actor 3) and Bert Jordine (Actor 1))

ACTOR 3: *(as Bob Cottingham)* There will be other clubs interested in you Laurie.

ACTOR 2: I'm glad you're so confident Bob.

ACTOR 1: Bob's right – of course there will.

ACTOR 2: Yeah – well – we'll see.

ACTOR 3: I've got a few irons in the fire – spoken to a few contacts.

ACTOR 2: I appreciate it.

ACTOR 3: In the meantime, though you've got to keep yourself fit – razor sharp and ready in case you get a trial somewhere.

ACTOR 1: He's doing that alright – aren't you Laurie?

ACTOR 2: I'm doing alright.

ACTOR 3: So, where are you training?

ACTOR 2: In my bedroom.

ACTOR 3: Your bedroom?

ACTOR 1: We practise all the moves in Laurie's bedroom.

ACTOR 3: What moves?

ACTOR 2: Dance moves.

ACTOR 3: Dance moves?

ACTOR 1: Are you a parrot or something – had too much Trill?

ACTOR 2: Bert and me go dancing – that's what we do – it's how I stay fit – that and a bit of Karate.

ACTOR 3: Dancing's not training.

ACTOR 2: It is for me.

ACTOR 3: Not football training – not like I used to put you through in the boys' team at Highgate.

ACTOR 2: All we did was run up and down the pitch – same as at Arsenal.

ACTOR 3: That's what you have to do –

ACTOR 2: If you want to be a boring drudge of a player – yeah – yeah – it's great – but that's not me.

ACTOR 3: I know but you can't let yourself go to seed.

ACTOR 2: I'm not – the reverse in fact – the dancing makes me light on my feet – quick almost instant changes of direction – shifts in tempo – balance – everything – every movement I make when I run at a defender – it's all there – that's what dancing's about.

ACTOR 1: Especially at the clubs we go to.

ACTOR 2: And the dance-offs – that's what really gets you going – gets the pulse racing like no football training's ever done.

ACTOR 1: And believe me – you want to see Laurie in the dance offs.

ACTOR 2: And when we showcase our moves

ACTOR 1: At the All Nations Club – London Fields.

ACTOR 2: The Bluesville in Wood Green.

ACTOR 1:   Crackers on Wardour Street's got the best scene

ACTOR 2:   The Best DJ's.

(The Actors become Laurie Cunningham (Actor 2), Bert Jordine (Actor 1) and DJ George Power (Actor 3) at the Bluesville)

ACTOR 3:   *(in DJ style rising to a crescendo like the announcer at a boxing match)* And good evening ladies and gentlemen - and this is George Power – your DJ for the next hour or two. Yes you 'acrobat-with-moves-off-pat-foot-tapping-rat-a-tat-tat-cool-cats' Crackers is where-it's-at! And tonight, we have a real-deal-disco-diva-fever-fest as Bert-the-heat-beat-jive-alive-Jordine and Laurie-whip-weavy-lash-flash-Cunningham – showcase their freestyle dazzle duo to the music Johnny Hammond and 'Fantasy'.

(Actors 2 & 3 now take it in turns to dance to Johnny Hammond's 'Fantasy')

ACTOR 1:   Have you ever witnessed such groovy-movie-hip-smoothies such curvy-kink-slinking and the sheer-swell-mell-decibel of your applause insures our thanks to our swerve-worthy-wonders: ladies and gentlemen of the Crackers' club – I give you – Cunningham and Jordine! *(Thunderous applause)*

(The Actors briefly become Leyton Orient fans on the terraces)

ALL: *(clapping and chanting) (Clap, clap, clap, clap, clap)*

Orient!

(Clap, clap, clap, clap, clap)

Orient!

(Clap, clap, clap, clap, clap)

Orient!

(Clap, clap, clap, clap, clap)

Orient!

(The Actors revert to become themselves)

ACTOR 1:   Leyton Orient – second division –

ACTOR 2:   And subject to much derision

ACTOR 3:   Especially from the fans of bigger clubs like West Ham,

(The Actors become West Ham fans)

ALL: *(singing as if West Ham fans to the tune of 'Go West')*
Sit down if you hate Orient
Sit down if you hate Orient
Sit down if you hate Orient
Sit down if you hate Orient

(The 3 Actors revert to become themselves)

ACTOR 1:   But in 72 – there's a new pride

Amongst Orient fans –

ACTOR 2:   As the Brisbane Road side

> Abandon crude 'kick and rush' for a fluent
> skilled game –

ACTOR 3: As the terraces sing out the new manager's name.

(The 3 Actors become Orient fans)

ALL: *(singing)* We love George Petchey oh yes we do,
We love George Petchey whate'er you do,
You are the Manager of our crew,
George Petchey we love you!

(The Actors now become George Petchey (Actor 3) the Manager at Leyton Orient, his Assistant Arthur Rowe (Actor 2) and Laurie Cunningham (Actor 1))

ACTOR 2: Where is he?

ACTOR 3: Don't get your bowels in an uproar Arthur.

ACTOR 2: Yeah but George – you pay me to train the team – coach them – get them ready for match days – how can I do that if Cunningham's never here on time?

ACTOR 3: He'll be here.

ACTOR 2: But not on time – I mean – he didn't even turn up on time for his trial. 'Overslept' – that's what he said – not that he ever says much.

ACTOR 3: He lets his feet do the talking for him.

ACTOR 2: He can't do that if he's not here.

ACTOR 3: Anything else?

ACTOR 2: I just wonder why you signed him.

ACTOR 3: He'll be here.

ACTOR 2: I'm not so sure.

ACTOR 3: I am – where that boy's concerned Arthur – I have every confidence.

(Actor 1 as Laurie Cunningham approaches)

ACTOR 2: And what time do you call this, eh?

ACTOR 3: Leave this to me Arthur.

ACTOR 2: You're the boss – but don't go soft on him.

(Pause)

ACTOR 3: And?

(Actor 1 shrugs)

ACTOR 3: Have you got nothing to say?

ACTOR 1: *(as Laurie Cunningham)* It wasn't my fault boss.

ACTOR 3: No?

ACTOR 1: I didn't wake up.

ACTOR 3: What about an alarm clock?

ACTOR 1: I still don't wake up.

ACTOR 3: So, I've got to send someone round to knock you up every morning have I?

37

ACTOR 1: I do my best boss.

ACTOR 3: So, do those boys out there training – but the difference is they're here on time Laurie.

ACTOR 1: They're nowhere near as fit as me and never will be however long they train.

ACTOR 3: That's not the point.

ACTOR 1: What's the point of training then if it's not to get fit?

ACTOR 3: So you need to train less than them – and that's why turning up late is fine for Laurie Cunningham - is that right?

ACTOR 1: Like I say boss – it's not my fault if I go to sleep and don't wake up.

ACTOR 3: I'm not talking about you Laurie – I know how fit you are – I know what you can do – I'm talking about them – out there – your teammates – and not one of them will ever be in your class no matter how many times they run up and down that pitch – I know that – I've got eyes – I've seen you play – but if you don't respect their time – the time they put in – the effort they make to be as good as they can be – then you don't respect them – and that means you don't respect me – and that hurts.

ACTOR 1: No – no – don't say that boss 'cos I do – I do.

ACTOR 3: Then show it – like I hope I show you – 'cos I've got the greatest admiration for you – for what

you are now and what I know you'll become –
not just as a footballer – but as a man Laurie –
'cos you could be as fine a man as you will be a
footballer and you're going to catch fire, son –
you're going to play for England.

(Pause as the impact of what has been said sinks in)

ACTOR 1:   I'm sorry Boss. I've let you down.

ACTOR 3:   Well here's what we're going to do: you earn £40
a week – yes?

ACTOR 1:   Yes.

ACTOR 3:   Every time you're even a second late from now
on I'm fining you £10.

ACTOR 1:   It won't happen again.

ACTOR 3:   I hope not – but just to make sure – I'm back
dating it to the beginning of this week – so you
owe me £30. Now we've got Millwall on Saturday
at the Den so get out there with the boys – 'cos
you're going to need them – believe me – you're
going to need all the support they can give you
and some more besides.

(The Actors become Millwall fans on the terraces)

ALL: *(Chanting)*

Millwall *(clap, clap, clap)*

Millwall *(clap, clap, clap)*

Millwall *(clap, clap, clap)*

(The Actors now become a Commentator/Cunningham and Millwall fans on the terraces)

ACTOR 1:   *(as the commentator and Cunningham)* And it's Heppolette to Fisher and on to Cunningham.

ACTORS 2 & 3:   *(as Millwall fans)* If you want to send him back clap your hands *(clap clap clap)*

ACTOR 1:   *(as the commentator and Cunningham)* And it's Cunningham's again - past Tony Hazell this time–

ACTORS 2 & 3:   If you want to send him back clap your hands *(clap clap clap)*

ACTOR 1:   *(as the commentator and Cunningham)* Past McGrath and Donaldson – it's as if they're simply not there – wonderful skill – simply wonderful.

ACTORS 2 & 3:   If you want to send him back – clap your hands *(clap, clap, clap)*

ACTOR 1:   *(as the commentator and Cunningham)* And this time it's Evans who's left foundering – Cunningham is on fire this afternoon.

ACTORS 2 & 3:   If you want to send them back stamp your feet *(stamp your feet)*

ACTOR 1:   *(as the commentator and Cunningham)* Goal! Cunningham hit that so sweetly - what a goal - what a performance - what a player -

ACTORS 2 & 3: If you want to send them back and get rid of every black

If you want to send them back stamp your feet. *(Stamp, stamp, stamp)*

(Actor 1 as Cunningham blows a kiss to the Millwall fans and then stands defiantly and gives a Black Power Salute to the crowd)

ACTORS 2 & 3: *(shouting angrily)* We'll get you Cunningham / you black bastard / you'll see / lynch him that's what I say / come on the KKK.

(The Actors become part of a press conference after the match)

ACTOR 1: Excuse me George but my readers would like to know if you feel any sense of responsibility for what happened out there on the pitch today.

ACTOR 2: So would mine! We nearly had a riot on our hands.

ACTOR 3: Why should I feel responsible for the Millwall fans' behaviour? I'm the manager of Leyton Orient.

ACTOR 2: There are some people who might say that your actions could have incited a riot.

ACTOR 1: And Cunningham – giving that black power salute when the final whistle blew.

ACTOR 1: Exactly and the Metropolitan Police Inspector I just interviewed says and I quote: 'Mr Petchey needs to think much more carefully about the teams he picks when he comes to venues like the Den.'

ACTOR 2: 'Provocative' is the word that I've heard bandied about.

ACTOR 3: I can't believe I'm hearing this.

ACTOR 2: Well let me spell it out: Cunningham, Fisher and Heppolette all in the same team.

ACTOR 3: Because they're good enough.

ACTOR 1: And what about the white boys -

ACTOR 3: What about them?

ACTOR 1: - the boys who are good enough to be on your books and were born in this country.

ACTOR 3: So was Cunningham born in this country and he ran rings round Millwall's all white boys this afternoon and all he got for his trouble was monkey chants and bananas thrown at him - and I'll bet you don't say a word about that in your match reports.

ACTOR 1: I didn't hear any chanting.

ACTOR 3: Nor me – nothing I don't usually hear.

ACTOR 2: No – no – you guys never do - any more than the referee or the linesmen or people from the FA – no-one ever hears anything – not officially anyway.

(The Actors become MP's in The House of Commons)

ACTOR 3:   *(as the Speaker)* Order! Order! The Home Secretary – The Right Honourable Roy Jenkins wishes to make a statement to the House.

ACTOR 1:   As I have already said before the first reading of this bill – the purpose of this legislation – The Race Relations Act 1976 – is to make provision with respect to discrimination on racial grounds and I say again what I have said many, many times before in this House - this vital piece of legislation – introduced by this Labour Government – *(cries of 'here, here' from the other Actors)* – will transform our society – eradicate prejudice and once and for all establish racial equality across this great country of ours.

ALL: Here! Here!

(The Actors become 2 Policemen and Laurie Cunningham)

ACTOR 1:   Where are you going son?

ACTOR 3:   Home.

ACTOR 2:   And where's that?

ACTOR 3:   Crouch Hill.

ACTOR 1:   Address?

ACTOR 3:   6 Tinder Road.

ACTOR 2:   So, what are you doing over here in the East End?

ACTOR 3:   I've been to training.

ACTOR 1: I've never heard it called that.

ACTOR 3: What?

ACTOR 1: Don't play the innocent with me son.

ACTOR 2: Name.

ACTOR 3: What's this about? Why are you stopping me?

ACTOR 1: *(with emphasis)* Name.

ACTOR 3: I haven't done anything.

ACTOR 2: That's what you all say.

ACTOR 1: *(with real aggression)* Name!

(Beat)

ACTOR 3: Laurie Cunningham.

ACTOR 2: Open the bag.

ACTOR 3: It's just my football kit.

ACTOR 1: Are you deaf or something – open it.

(He opens the bag)

ACTOR 2: *(examining the contents)* What's this then?

ACTOR 3: Football boots.

ACTOR 1: Where do you get these then?

ACTOR 3: They're mine.

ACTOR 1: Two pairs?

ACTOR 3:   I'm a footballer – that's what I do.

ACTOR 2:   And I'm a bleeding ballet dancer.

ACTOR 3:   No – no – no honestly –

ACTOR 2:   You wouldn't know the meaning of the word.

ACTOR 1:   You're coming with us.

ACTOR 3:   Why?

ACTOR 2:   On suspicion.

ACTOR 3:   Of what?

ACTOR 1:   Intent to commit an arrestable offence.

ACTOR 3:   What offence?

ACTOR 2:   That's what we're going to find out.

ACTOR 1:   That's what the Sus Law's for –

ACTOR 2:   So, people like us can keep people like you in check.

(The Actors combine as a radio commentator)

ACTOR 1:   And as play gets under way here for the second half in this second division tie between Orient and Fulham on this freezing cold February afternoon –

ACTOR 2:   The score at nil all gives no indication of the way Orient or should I say Laurie Cunningham has dominated their London rivals –

ACTOR 3:   And it's Fisher with the ball – *(Actors 1 & 2 boo)* – and the boos rise for the black player just as they did in the first half from the Fulham fans in the East Stand –

ACTOR 1:   *(as he begins to speak Actors 2&3 boo)* And they're even louder now as Fisher threads the ball through to Cunningham and what a precision pass that was –

ACTOR 2:   Here he goes again –

ACTOR 3:   You can feel the electricity in the crowd as he gets the ball.

ACTOR 1:   What's he going to do this time?

ALL: Laurie Cunningham.

(The Actors now simultaneously give the commentary and become Cunningham moving in stylised synchronicity)

ACTOR 2:   Twisting –

ACTOR 1:   Turning –

ACTOR 2:   This way –

ACTOR 3:   Then that –

ACTOR 3:   Piercing the Fulham defence at will –

ACTOR 2:   Such balance –

ACTOR 1:   Control –

ACTOR 3:   Such skill on the ball

(Beat)

ACTOR 1: *(upping the tempo)* A turn of pace –

ACTOR 2: Like the crack of a gun -

ACTOR 3: A darting run left –

ACTOR 1: Then a feint –

ACTOR 2: And a swerve –

ACTOR 3: Curving an arc –

ACTOR 2: With just Bobby Moore in his path to goal –

ACTOR 1: Steps in –

ACTOR 2: Glides out –

ACTOR 3: Beyond Moore's reach -

ACTOR 1: The final breach in the Fulham line –

ACTOR 2: *(rising anticipation)* One flashing glance –

ACTOR 3: A moment's chance to target spot – and –

ALL: Crack!

ACTOR 2: The bullet's fired!

(The Actors now stop their synchronised moving and simply commentate)

ALL: Goal!

ACTOR 3: The crowd erupts –

ACTOR 2: The winning score!

ALL: Laurie Cunningham.

ACTOR 1:   The way he went past Bobby Moore – only Pele or Best could surpass that.

ACTOR 3:   He's a rare find.

ACTOR 2:   He's in a different class.

(The Actors become Laurie Cunningham, Bobby Fisher and George Petchey)

ACTOR 3:   I'm so proud of you two boys.

ACTOR 2:   Cheers boss.

ACTOR 1:   Yeah – we moved the ball around well –

ACTOR 2:   Kept it flowing like you said.

ACTOR 3:   That's not what I mean

ACTOR 1:   What then?

ACTOR 3:   You showed 'em – those bigoted bloody fans – didn't matter what they did – how many bananas they threw on the pitch – the booing – the chanting – you showed 'em.

ACTOR 2:   We didn't do anything.

ACTOR 3:   Oh yes you did Laurie – and you Bobby – you played brilliant football and that's what did the talking – no need for the other stuff – winding them up with fisted salutes and what-not – it's your football that got to them – showing them

48

just how good you are – best players on the field
– Laurie Cunningham and Bobby Fisher –

ACTOR 1: Thanks boss.

ACTOR 2: Yeah thanks – it means a lot.

ACTOR 3: It's true – you were the best players out there by a country mile and that's what made their fans turn so ugly – and that's what anyone with eyes can't fail to see – the better you boys played – the uglier they got – and that's how you'll win – in the long run – that's how you'll do it – show them up for what they are through the beauty of your game – the beauty and the style.

(The Actors revert to become themselves)

ACTOR 1: But this boy's mind style is not confined to white lined pitches –

ACTOR 2: Not bound to inducing a round leather ball to do his will – to spin and curve – in tight control –

ACTOR 3: His soul's voice cries 'improvise' –

ACTOR 1: Variety –

ACTOR 2: Surprise –

ACTOR 3: Suspense –

ACTOR 1: Whether running at the opposition defence or going out to dance

ACTOR 2: Everything –

ACTOR 3:   Everything is a chance to shake things up –

(The Actors become 3 Laurie Cunningham's preparing for a night out)

ACTOR 3:   It's Tuesday night – so it might be blues –

ACTOR 1:   Or Ska –

ACTOR 2:   Or a reggae band –

ACTOR 3:   Or at Global Village down on The Strand –

ACTOR 1:   We can dance till dawn to soul –

ACTOR 2:   Or punk –

ACTOR 3:   Or there's hard funk on Jermyn Street.

ACTOR 2:   At the Purple Pussycat there's American beat and jive and rock.

ACTOR 1:   At Crackers you get a total mix –

ACTOR 2:   You can 'take-your-pick how you dance or dress or wear your hair –

ACTOR 3:   Not trapped in some stereotype –

ACTOR 1:   Without a key to unlock variety when you fancy it –

(Actor 1 begins dressing as Laurie in the Gatsby style – Music Peter Herbolzheimer Rhythm Combination & Brass – Jive Samba)

ACTOR 1:   Sometimes it's the loose fit of the Oxford bags –

The double breasted wide flapped suit –

50

The sparkling sheen of shoes and spats –

The angle of the Fedora hat –

The Gatsby look – perfect – complete.

For a night on Oxford Street at the 100 Club –

The suit – straight off the pages

Of a fashion magazine from the Jazz Age –

(Actor 2 begins dressing as Laurie in the Funk style. Music - Play That Funky Music by Wild Cherry)

ACTOR 2:   But sometimes it's a different page from a different book –

A reinvented look and fashion

For a night of funk –

Clashing colours –

Shirts open necked –

The broadest stripes or even broader checks –

With Cuban heels –

And tight hipped flairs –

Dark shades and Afro hair combed to candy floss–

'Cos Maunkberry's won't admit no dross – only the best dressed are in the queue –

(Actor 3 begins dressing as Laurie in the Soul Boy style – Music Young Hearts Run Free Candi Staton)

ACTOR 3:   But then again Casual Soul Boy might emerge

If the urge takes you –

With the retro blue shirt, untucked with short sleeves –

And carpenter-style, baggy jeans,

And flat soled shoes complete the look

Of another page in another book.

(Beat)

ACTOR 1:   *(speaking direct to the audience)* It was the casual soul look that our boy wore one Sunday in 1975–

ACTOR 2:   A jazz jive night at the Tottenham Royal -

ACTOR 3:   Hoping to see the girl he'd spoken to the week before –

ACTOR 1:   He was scanning the dance floor and the bar - when...

(The Actors become Nikki Hare-Brown, Laurie Cunningham and the Voice of Commentary who addresses the audience directly)

ACTOR 2:   *(as Nikki)* You're a liar!

ACTOR 1:   *(as The Voice of Commentary direct to the audience)* The young girl said sounding angry.

ACTOR 3:	*(as Laurie Cunningham and clearly taken aback)* Sorry?
ACTOR 2:	You heard me.
ACTOR 1:	Very angry!
ACTOR 2:	I'm talking about last week.
ACTOR 1:	Angry – and – and – well – no getting away from it – white – the girl was white.
ACTOR 2:	You told me your name was Paul.
ACTOR 1:	*(direct to the audience)* Long fair hair.
ACTOR 3:	I never did.
ACTOR 1:	Piercing blue eyes.
ACTOR 2:	Why would I say it then?
ACTOR 1:	*(direct to the audience)* And attitude.
ACTOR 3:	Search me.
ACTOR 1:	*(direct to the audience)* Loads of attitude.
ACTOR 2:	No need – the police will probably do that on your way home.
ACTOR 3:	Thanks for that.
ACTOR 2:	Serves you right if they do.
ACTOR 3:	Like I say – 'thanks'.
ACTOR 2:	Anyway I know what your real name is. Your name's Laurie.

ACTOR 3:	Wow! I never knew that.
ACTOR 2:	I recognised you on the telly playing football – and they kept saying your name – it's Laurie – not Paul.
ACTOR 3:	I never said it was Paul.
ACTOR 2:	And you never said it wasn't.
ACTOR 3:	I don't follow the logic.
ACTOR 1:	But logic had nothing to do with this.
ACTOR 2:	That's what was on your shirt.
ACTOR 1:	This was chemistry.
ACTOR 3:	Paul?
ACTOR 2:	On your shirt –
ACTOR 1:	Chemistry pure and simple.
ACTOR 2:	It was embroidered on the breast pocket - the word 'Paul'. I noticed it.
ACTOR 1:	She'd noticed alright.
ACTOR 3:	Oh yeah – yeah I remember –
ACTOR 1:	She'd noticed quite a bit
ACTOR 3:	On the breast pocket – yeah –
ACTOR 1:	But then again – so had he –
ACTOR 3:	I bought it on the Kings Road –

ACTOR 1:   They'd noticed each other.

ACTOR 3:   I liked the style.

ACTOR 2:   Do you mean the retro shop.

ACTOR 3:   Oh – you know it do you?

ACTOR 2:   Course I do.

(The Actors become Arthur Rowe George Petchey and Laurie Cunningham. Arthur and Petchey are at the football club and Laurie Cunningham is deep in conversation with Nikki who is not seen)

ACTOR 1:   *(as Arthur)* I'm seriously worried about that boy George.

ACTOR 3:   *(as George Petchey)* No need to worry Arthur.

ACTOR 1:   I'm amazed you can't see it boss.

ACTOR 3:   What is there to see?

ACTOR 1:   Ever since he met that girl.

ACTOR 3:   Nikki's a nice kid and she's smart.

ACTOR 1:   Too bloody smart – it's like his mind's somewhere else.

(They freeze as Cunningham begins his apparent conversation with Nikki one Summer night on the roof of her parent's house)

ACTOR 2:   *(as Cunningham)* I love sitting up here Nikki – looking at the stars – I love it – it's like – like we're so small – it's frightening how small – insignificant pin pricks compared to what's that's out there – I mean – look – look – everywhere – so much – so many stars – and what's that one again – there – you can see it clearly tonight – so clear – that constellation – you know – the one you told me about last time – *(pointing)* – the one there – shaped like an eagle – what's it called?

(Actor 2 freezes)

ACTOR 1:   He's not like the other boys boss.

ACTOR 3:   I'm not sure that's such a bad thing.

ACTOR 1:   Of course it is – they all do stuff together after training - go for a game of snooker or a round of golf – that sort of thing - does them good.

ACTOR 3:   It's not Laurie's bag and never has been.

ACTOR 1:   He could try.

ACTOR 3:   He's in love Arthur.

ACTOR 1:   He could still try.

(Actors 1 & 3 freeze)

ACTOR 2:   *(as before looking up at the stars)* And to think that all those years ago - how many was it – two – three thousand - more than that maybe – to think people alive then were looking up at that same sky – at the same constellation – 'cos they were – they must have been – 'cos they saw the same shape that we see – Aquila the Eagle – up there in the sky – and came up with the story you

56

told me about him being the carrier of Zeus' thunderbolts. I love that story – I'd like to come up with things like that – stories – poems – I love poems.

(Actor 2 freezes)

ACTOR 1:   He's got his head in the clouds George – and the shit he talks – none of us know what he's on about half the time.

ACTOR 3:   Arthur – have you ever considered that what you just said then speaks more about us than it does him?

(Actors 1 & 3 freeze)

ACTOR 2:   I know – before we go in shall we just try those opening steps again – the ones from the Fred Astaire and Ginger Rogers routine.

(Actor 2 briefly dances the opening steps danced by Fred Astaire from a sequence in Top Hat 1935)

ACTOR 1:   We'll just have to agree to differ where Cunningham's concerned George and that's all there is to it.

ACTOR 3:   The way he plays is the way he lives Arthur and his football is brilliant so what does that tell us about his life?

ACTOR 1:   It'll all end in tears.

ACTOR 3:   Christ! You are a miserable bastard Arthur.

ACTOR 1:   A realist!

ACTOR 3:   Well here's some realism for you: that boys beyond any coaching we can give him – so thank your lucky stars the other players aren't as good 'cos if they were we'd both be out of a job. And anyway, my guess is he won't be with us much longer – a couple more games like he's played recently and the big boys will be coming for him.

(The Actors become George Petchey and 2 football journalists at a press conference)

ACTOR 1:   So George – how do you feel about losing your best player?

ACTOR 3:   Sorry to see him go – naturally – but I'm pleased for the boy – very pleased.

ACTOR 2:   And what about Leyton Orient?

ACTOR 3:   That's the way the game works. Clubs like us – we can't hold players back – not when they're as good as Laurie Cunningham – 'cos he's going to play for England – you see if I'm not right – he could even be the first black player to do so – but he won't do that here at Orient. He's got to play in the top division.

ACTOR 1:   Maybe but £115,000 is still a lot of money to pay for a player.

ACTOR 3:   Yeah and it's a lot of player they're getting. So, if you like a bit of a flutter have a punt on West Bromwich Albion coming in the top three at the very least – either this season or the next – you watch – that boy's just a bit special.

(The Actors become Dave Sexton, Laurie Cunningham and the Voice of Commentary who addresses the audience directly)

ACTOR 2:   Birmingham – April 1st 1977.

ACTOR 3:   May I speak to Laurie Cunningham please?

ACTOR 1:   Speaking.

ACTOR 3:   It's Dave Sexton here.

ACTOR 1:   And I'm Bob Marley – come on – who is it?

ACTOR 3:   Dave Sexton.

ACTOR 2:   It really is Dave Sexton.

ACTOR 1:   Shit! Sorry –

ACTOR 2:   The Manager of Manchester United

ACTOR 1:   I thought – um – er

ACTOR 2:   And of the England Under 21 side –

ACTOR 1:   I thought – er – I don't know what I thought

ACTOR 2:   He thought it was an April Fool joke.

ACTOR 3:   I hope you don't mind me ringing you.

ACTOR 1:   No – no – shit – no – no – not all.

ACTOR 3:   Well first of all congratulations on your move to Albion – I understand it's going well.

ACTOR 2:   Two goals on his home debut against Ipswich.

ACTOR 1:   Not too bad – thanks.

ACTOR 3:   And secondly and more to the point –

ACTOR 2:   The moment has come –

ACTOR 3:   I've picked you for the England Under 21 side –

ACTOR 2:   The first black player!

ACTOR 3:   The match is against Scotland.

ACTOR 2:   The first to represent England professionally at any level.

ACTOR 1:   April 27th – Bramall Lane –

(The 3 Actors become footballers standing in a team line before a match. God Save the Queen is played)

ALL: *(singing half-heartedly over the music and to the National Anthem)*

God save our gracious Queen,
Long live our noble Queen,
God Save the Queen.
Send her victorious,
Happy and glorious,
Long to reign over us,
God Save the Queen.

(The three players become England U21 footballers and Voices of Journalists reporting on the match. They initially line up as if for the kick-off of the match. A whistle blows and all 3 actors move into different positions illustrating an attacking football move and immediately freeze)

ACTOR 1:   *(speaking like a journalist ringing in a newspaper column on the instant the Actors freeze)* You

60

sensed the anticipation across the half empty
terraces each time Cunningham took possession
– the kind of electricity that used to be generated
by men like Jimmy Greaves.

*(A whistle blows again and the Actors move immediately into
different positions illustrating an attacking football move and
immediately freeze)*

ACTOR 2:   *(speaking like a journalist ringing in a newspaper
column)* Someone special has come amongst us -
Cunningham excites me more than anyone I can
remember.

*(A whistle blows again and the Actors move immediately into
different positions illustrating an attacking football move and
immediately freeze)*

ACTOR 3:   *(speaking like a journalist ringing in a newspaper
column)* Cunningham offers relief from a game
that has become pathetically about blood, sweat
and predictability.

*(A whistle blows again and the Actors – all as Laurie
Cunningham – in synchronised movement take a step forward and
kick an imaginary ball with power into a goal. At the sound of the
roar of the crowd celebrating a goal the 3 Actors simultaneously
raise both arms in triumph)*

*(The Actors become The Board of Directors at West Bromwich
Albion addressing the audience as if they are players sitting in a
dressing room)*

ACTOR 1: Now gentlemen you'll excuse us for coming in to your dressing room uninvited as it were - before you go out to train -

ACTOR 2: But we're here as Members of the Board to put things straight –

ACTOR 3: Clear things up –

ACTOR 1: 'Cos we know there's been a bit of turmoil recently at the club –

ACTOR 2: Two managers leaving in the space of six months and that sort of thing –

ACTOR 3: And we don't you thinking there's a crisis –

ACTOR 1: That we haven't got our fingers on the pulse –

ACTOR 2: Our hands on the tiller –

ACTOR 3: And our irons in the fire –

ACTOR 1: And we don't want you thinking we're not committed to this club –

ACTOR 2: 100% committed.

ACTOR 3: 150% in fact.

ACTOR 2: 'Cos we've signed new players –

ACTOR 3: Young Cunningham over there

ACTOR 1: And Regis – sat beside him.

ACTOR 2: And it's cost us a pretty penny I can tell you.

ACTOR 3: A lot of brass –

ACTOR 1:   So now we're looking for a return on our not inconsiderable investment –

ACTOR 2:   So, to see us through what remains of the 1978 season –

ACTOR 1:   And to take the ship forward –

ACTOR 3:   Pick up the reins –

ACTOR 1:   And fly the West Bromwich Albion kite – so to speak –

ACTOR 2:   We have appointed a new manager -

ACTOR 3:   Mr Ron Atkinson –

ALL: Big Ron!

(The Actors instantly become Ron Atkinson and 2 Voices of Commentary)

ACTOR 1:   Right lads – I know you will all be delighted –

ACTOR 2:   *(direct to the audience)* Big Ron's first training talk to the squad -

ACTOR 1:   - That I've brought with me from Cambridge United one of my players –

ACTOR 3:   *(direct to the audience)* A solid right back and Cambridge's captain –

ACTOR 1:   And here he is – this is Brendon Batson –

ACTOR 2:   *(direct to the audience)* That's three black players –

ACTOR 3:   (*direct to the audience*) No club had more –

ACTOR 1:   And that completes the jigsaw for our team –

ACTOR 2:   (*direct to the audience*) And so to the vision –

(The Actors all now become Ron Atkinson)

ACTOR 1:   I want you all to dream of success –

ACTOR 2:   I want you to go out and express yourselves –

ACTOR 3:   Play with passion –

ACTOR 1:   Invention –

ACTOR 2:   Flair –

ACTOR 3:   And the crowd will share in your excitement –

ACTOR 1:   'Cos that's why they come –

ACTOR 2:   That's why they've paid –

ACTOR 3:   They stand on those terraces to be entertained on a Saturday –

ACTOR 1:   'Cos Monday to Friday – what have they got with the state of the nation –

ACTOR 2:   Rampant inflation –

ACTOR 3:   Jobs under threat –

ACTOR 2:   Pay restraint –

ACTOR 1:   And debt as high as the rubbish piling up in mounds –

64

ACTOR 2:   In towns and cities across the land –

ACTOR 3:   As growing hatred is fanned by voices hell bent

On exploiting the winter of discontent and discord –

(The 3 Actors become John Tyndall and his associates at The National Front Conference of 1978)

ACTOR 1:   And now ladies and gentlemen to close our 1978 Party Conference it is our pleasure to introduce our leader –

ACTOR 2:   The man who formed this great party of ours –

ACTOR 1:   The man who led us so gloriously just a few months ago in The Battle of Lewisham –

ACTOR 2:   The man who showed not a morsel fear in the face of all those liberal lefty lackies trying to stop our legitimate right to march on streets that are ours by birth –

ACTOR 1:   Ladies and gentlemen – the founder of your party –

ACTOR 2:   Britain's party –

ACTOR 2:   The leader of The National Front – Mr John Tyndall –

(There is the sound of rapturous applause – Music – Ghost Town The Specials)

ACTOR 3:   *(as John Tyndall)* What does multiculturalism mean to the white world? Nothing except division, disunity, weakness, and failure. Five of your beautiful daughters are in the hands of foreigners – London, Liverpool, Bradford, Burnley and Birmingham. The foreigners are doing to your daughters as they will. The daughters are crying for help, and the white world is silent. And some of them are collaborating with the rape of these five beautiful white daughters. Why? Because they are too weak and too corrupt to do anything about it. So, this is what multiculturalism will do to the whites. Are you ready to have another hundred years like the forty years you just had?

(There is more rapturous applause)

(The Actors become 3 Editors at The BBC - Match of The Day music)

ACTOR 1:   So, what else have we got for tonight's programme?

ACTOR 2:   Something interesting.

ACTOR 3:   There's some footage of the Albion team bus arriving at Goodison Park.

ACTOR 1:   Why would anyone want to watch that?

ACTOR 2:   Exactly – it's not as if we're not showing highlights of the match.

ACTOR 1:   And that's all anyone in football wants to see.

ACTOR 3:   Well – maybe they should widen their horizons a bit.

ACTOR 2:	And show them a team bus pulling up a football ground!
ACTOR 3:	This is a bit different.
ACTOR 1:	In what way?
ACTOR 3:	The abuse.
ACTOR 2:	That's hardly news –
ACTOR 3:	You need to look the footage.
ACTOR 1:	Away teams always get stick from home fans - we all know that.
ACTOR 3:	These aren't just home fans.
ACTOR 2:	Who is it then?
ACTOR 3:	The National Front – the banners and placards are clear to see – and the verbal abuse – the chanting – the spitting – well – I've never seen anything like it.
ACTOR 1:	Send it to one of the political programme producers then. Let them deal with it.
ACTOR 2:	I agree – our viewers don't want us taking a political stance.
ACTOR 1:	We have to be objective –
ACTOR 2:	It's in the BBC Charter –
ACTOR 1:	We can't show bias –
ACTOR 3:	The camera doesn't lie –

ACTOR 2: I'll bet it was only shot from one angle though – there are always two sides to any story.

ACTOR 3: So, you're not going to have a look.

ACTOR 1: I've already told you – I've made up my mind –

ACTOR 3: Without seeing it!

ACTOR 2: We don't need to see it.

ACTOR 3: We're as bad as they are – those racist bastards in the footage – they've all made up their minds as well.

ACTOR 1: You'd better watch what you say.

ACTOR 3: Somebody's got to say something.

ACTOR 2: Maybe so – but not us. That's not our job.

ACTOR 1: Nor is upsetting the viewers -

ACTOR 2: Or the FA come to that -

ACTOR 1: Or the clubs –

ACTOR 2: Especially the clubs –

ACTOR 1: Without their support we wouldn't have a programme - there'd be no Match of The Day.

ACTOR 2: And like I say – it's the only the away matches that this happens – the home crowd at The Hawthorns love their three blacks

(The Actors become Laurie, Nikki and Racist Drunks outside a nightclub – Music – Gangsters The Specials)

ACTOR 1: *(as the Racist Drunk)* Oi – you –

ACTOR 2: *(as Nikki)* Ignore him Laurie –

ACTOR 1: I'm talking to you 'Blackie' –

ACTOR 2: Just ignore him.

(Actor 1 now blocks Actor 3's way)

ACTOR 1: So, where do you think you're going then?

ACTOR 2: Let's just go back into the club.

ACTOR 1: *(positioning himself so Laurie cannot retreat)* You're going nowhere. (Beat) And is this your girlfriend?

ACTOR 2: Just leave us alone alright.

ACTOR 1: You what?

ACTOR 2: We don't want any trouble.

ACTOR 1: Well you've got it – like it or not.

ACTOR 3: Back off mate.

ACTOR 1: What did you say?

ACTOR 2: *(quietly)* Leave this to me Laurie.

ACTOR 1: I asked you what you just said.

ACTOR 3: He didn't say anything.

ACTOR 1: Bollocks!

ACTOR 3: That's enough of that.

ACTOR 1: And who's going to stop me?

ACTOR 2: Like I say – ignore him - he's not worth it.

ACTOR 1: Worth a fuck sight more than you – you nigger lover.

ACTOR 3: That's it.

ACTOR 2: No!

ACTOR 3: Stay out of this Nikki – I've had enough of this prick.

ACTOR 2: Please don't.

ACTOR 1: I'll bet you never say 'don't' to him.

(Laurie very deftly throws the Drunk Racist to the ground and pins him down and lifts his head as if to bang it on the pavement. He is stopped by Nikki's intervention)

ACTOR 2: No Laurie – stop – stop – please Laurie – don't – just let him go – do you hear me Laurie?

ACTOR 1: *(still pinned to the ground)* You're not that 'Laurie' are you – you know – Laurie Cunningham.

ACTOR 3: What of it?

ACTOR 1: Why didn't you say? I'm a 'Baggies' fan - I love you mate – you and the other boys – Cyrille and Brendon – you're bloody brilliant – all three of you – you've transformed the Albion –

(Laurie releases him without offering any acknowledgement)

ACTOR 3: Come on Nikki - let's go home.

ACTOR 1: *(calling after them)* Sorry about the misunderstanding Laurie – still no harm done eh – *(beat)* – and all the best over there in Spain against Valencia in the EUEFA Cup next week! I only wish I had a ticket. *(Beat)* Eh! I don't suppose you could get one for us!

(The 3 Actors revert to become themselves)

ACTOR 1: Two matches define his era -

ACTOR 2: When football came as near to perfection as life allows –

ACTOR 3: And three black players took their bows not as chorus nor in minor roles -

ACTOR 1: But centre stage –

ACTOR 2: The head, heart and soul of the assembled company.

ACTOR 3: First the UEFA Cup third round –

ACTOR 1: West Bromwich Albion are away to mighty Valencia in Spain.

(The 3 Actors become increasingly emotional Spanish Commentators and describe the action with synchronised but ever more dramatic gesticulations)

ACTOR 1: Y aquí estamos en el Mastella Stadium de Valencia para el partido de ida de la tercera ronda de la Copa de la UEFA –

ACTOR 2: Los gigantes españoles Valencia contra el humilde West Bromwich Albion de Birmingham, Inglaterra –

ACTOR 3: Y con la puntuación a una cero en Valencia, es Laurie Cunningham con el balón, y pasa volando por Carete como si no estuviera allí –

ACTOR 1: Solo Kempes en su camino –

ACTOR 2: Kempes, el mejor jugador del mundo, ganador de The Golden Boot en La Copa del Mundo de este verano en Argentina.

ACTOR 3: Y – ¡Dios mío! ¡Cunningham tiene fuego en sus botas!

ACTOR 2: Ha dejado a Kempes por muerto.

ACTOR 3: Es un toque para Brown y para volve a Cunningham – y – y – y

ACTOR 1: Qué disparo!

ACTOR 2: ¡Vaya objetivo!

ACTOR 3: ¡Qué jugador! Laurie Cunningham!

ACTOR 1: ¡La perla Negra!

ACTOR 2: ¡La estrella del show!

ACTOR 3: El pequeño maestro!

ALL: Pura perfección – Laurie Cunningham!

(And here we are at The Mastella Stadium Valencia for the first leg of the third round of The UEFA Cup – Spanish giants

Valencia versus the humble West Bromwich Albion from Birmingham England. And with the score at one nil to Valencia it is Laurie Cunningham with the ball – and he flies past Carete as if he wasn't there – only Kempes in his path – Kempes – the Best Player in the world – winner of The Golden Boot in this Summer's World Cup in Argentina. And – oh my goodness! Cunningham has fire in his boots! He has left Kempes for dead. It's one touch to Brown and back to Cunningham – and – and – and – what a shot! What a goal! What a player! Laurie Cunningham! The Black Pearl! The star of the show! The little master! Pure perfection – Laurie Cunningham)

(The Actors become Laurie Cunningham, Cyrille Regis and Brendon Batson on the pitch at Old Trafford and looking in awe around the stadium)

ACTOR 1: This is it then boys – Old Trafford –

ACTOR 2: The 'Theatre of Dreams' –

ACTOR 3: Just wait for the roar when we walk out here with our teammates –

ACTOR 1: So, take it all in – 'cos in an hour or so –

ACTOR 2: Seventy-five thousand will stack these stands –

ACTOR 3: In one teeming pack –

ACTOR 2: Baying for blood –

ACTOR 1: Ours especially –

ACTOR 3: Especially ours –

ACTOR 2: Especially us three.

(The Actors become the Manchester United crowd)

ALL: Glory glory Man United

                          Glory glory Man United

                          Glory glory Man United

                          And the Reds go marching on -

(The Actors now alternate in synchronised movements between being Cunningham / Regis / Batson whilst simultaneously commentating on themselves and Manchester United Fans booing, doing 'monkey chants' and throwing bananas)

ALL: *(commentating and moving as if Cunningham)*
                          And Cunningham picks up the ball in midfield

(The Actors become Man United fans booing)

ALL: Booooooooooo!

(The Actors become Regis simultaneously commentating)

ALL: *(commentating and moving as if Regis) A perfectly weighted pass to Regis - who back heels it - what a deft touch -*

(The Actors become Man United fans doing 'Monkey Chants' together with the actions)

ALL: Ooh! Ooh! Ooh! Ooh! Ooh!

(The Actors become Batson simultaneously commentating)

ALL: *(commentating and moving as if Batson)* And that's how to time a tackle – and Batson comes

away with the ball and strokes it inch perfect
into the path of Cunningham – and he's flying!

*(The Actors become Man United fans singing and throwing
bananas)*

ALL: *(singing)* If you fancy a fruity treat
                 Unzip a banana.

*(As they sing the word 'banana' they throw an imaginary piece of
fruit towards the pitch in a synchronised movement)*

*(The Actors now all become Commentators with rapid fire
delivery)*

ACTOR 1:   Cunningham through the middle – crosses –

ALL: Goal

ACTOR 2:   Batson to Cunningham to Regis –

ALL: Goal!

ACTOR 3:   Cunningham comes again –

ALL: Goal! Goal! Goal!

*(The Actors become Albion fans singing back to Manchester
United fans)*

ALL: *(singing)* You're not booing now –
                 You're not booing now –
                 Ee ay addio
                 You're not booing now!

(The 3 Actors become Cunningham, Batson and Regis)

ACTOR 1:   *(as Cyrille Regis)* So what do you reckon of the idea then Brendon?

ACTOR 2:   *(as Brendon Batson)* I think it's ridiculous – I think it's humiliating.

ACTOR 1:   It's only a bit of fun.

ACTOR 2:   Oh, come on Cyrille – it's a cheap publicity stunt – that's all it is.

ACTOR 1:   It can't do us any harm.

ACTOR 2:   It's not about us –

ACTOR 1:   Who then?

ACTOR 2:   Who do you think – who came up with the idea in the first place? It sure as hell wasn't them – I mean – can you imagine? *(He parodies The Three Degrees in conversation)* I'll tell you what girls when we get to England the first thing we must do after making use of our brand new hair straighteners is fly straight up to Birmingham – to that dinky little football club we've all heard so much about – West Bromwich Albion – and have our photographs taken with those three beautiful big black boys who are all the rage - Now I don't care what you say – it's an opportunity too great to miss - and we gotta go even if it does mean missing the special concert we're doing for Prince Charles.'

ACTOR 1:   That's really funny Brendon!

ACTOR 2: Yeah but the point is – those Three Degree girls have never heard of us – why would they want their picture taken with us – this is all Big Ron's idea – it's all about his ego –

ACTOR 1: Everything's about Big Ron's ego – but that's not a reason not to do the photoshoot.

ACTOR 2: Can't you see we're being used?

ACTOR 1: How come?

ACTOR 2: Like – like – we're some kind of novelty act –

ACTOR 1: I don't care – I fancy the idea.

ACTOR 2: We all know what you fancy Cyrille?

ACTOR 1: Nothing wrong having a bit of a laugh.

ACTOR 2: Not if it's at our expense.

(Beat)

ACTOR 1: What do you think Laurie?

ACTOR 2: Yeah come on Laurie – you haven't said a word.

Actor 3: I think Brendon's pretty much right – a novelty act – that's what this is all about – yeah – yeah – I agree with that.

ACTOR 2: So, you don't want to do it either.

ACTOR 3: I didn't say that.

ACTOR 1: What are you saying then?

ACTOR 3: I think maybe we should do it.

ACTOR 2: Laurie – you are making no sense – no sense at all.

ACTOR 3: Ok – well – I guess what I'm saying is you have to start somewhere.

ACTOR 2: By having the piss taken out of us.

ACTOR 1: That happens anyway.

ACTOR 3: Cyrille's right.

ACTOR 2: Now you're just sitting on the fence.

ACTOR 3: No, I'm not – we have the piss taken every time we walk on the pitch.

ACTOR 2: This is different.

ACTOR 1: How?

ACTOR 2: We know what we're doing on a football pitch – we're footballers – that's our world.

ACTOR 3: That's not how they think though is it – the fans who boo us and throw bananas at us. They don't think we belong on the football pitch.

ACTOR 1: As far as they're concerned, we don't belong anywhere.

ACTOR 3: And all the while we go along with that – on the football pitch – or anywhere you like – all the while we say – 'oh we can't go there – politics – or showbiz – or whatever – we can't do that it's not our world' – all the while we say that – it never will be our world – that's what I mean when I say 'you have to start somewhere.'

ACTOR 1:   So, what do you reckon then Brendon?

(The 3 Actors now become The Three Degrees singing When Will I see You Again)

ALL: *(singing)* Hoo-oo ha-a ha-a hoo-oo
Precious moments
When will I see you again
When will we share precious moments
Will I have to wait forever
Will I have to suffer
And cry the whole night through?

(The 3 Actors become PFA Officials and The England Football Manager Ron Greenwood at the 1978/79 PFA Annual Dinner and Award Ceremony)

ACTOR 1:   *(as a PFA Official announcing awards)* And ladies and gentlemen we now come to that part of the evening when we announce The Professional Football Association's Team of the Year.

ACTOR 2:   *(as the second PFA Official announcing awards)* Now this award is regarded as by far the most significant honour that any footballer can receive aside from international recognition -

ACTOR 1:   - because this award is of course voted for by the professional players themselves –

ACTOR 2:   And what greater distinction can be than knowing you have won the admiration of your fellow professionals.

ACTOR 1:   So, without more ado to announce the names of the PFA Team of the Year for 1978/79 season – the England football manager –

ACTOR 2:   Mr Ron Greenwood –

(Actor 3 steps forward as Ron Greenwood)

ACTOR 1:   Number One and Number Two both from Nottingham Forest –

ACTOR 3:   Peter Shilton and Viv Anderson

ACTOR 2:   Numbers Three and Four from Arsenal and Manchester City –

ACTOR 3:   David O'Leary and Dave Watson –

ACTOR 1:   Numbers 5 and 6 from West Bromwich Albion and Arsenal

ACTOR 3:   Derek Statham and Liam Brady

ACTOR 2:   Numbers 7 and 8 from Leeds United and Tottenham

ACTOR 3:   Tony Currie and Osvaldo Ardiles –

ACTOR 1:   Numbers 9 and 10 from West Bromwich Albion and Liverpool

ACTOR 3:   Cyrille Regis and Kenny Dalglish –

ACTOR 2:   And last but by no mean least – number 11 from West Bromwich Albion –

ACTOR 3:   Laurie Cunningham –

ACTOR 1:   Who we'd also like to congratulate on selection to make his full England against Wales at Wembley in just two weeks' time –

ACTOR 2:   Only the second black player ever to win a full England cap – well done Laurie.

ACTOR 1:   My word how things have changed Ron!

ACTOR 3:   *(with huge smugness)* No-one can accuse the football hierarchy of racism anymore!

(The 3 Actors become Laurie Cunningham, Ron Atkinson and Bert Millichip)

ACTOR 1:   *(as Ron Atkinson)* Come in Laurie – come in – son –

ACTOR 2:   Thanks boss –

ACTOR 1:   Have a cigar.

ACTOR 2:   No thanks boss – I don't smoke.

ACTOR 1:   You don't mind if we do?

ACTOR 2:   Not at all boss.

ACTOR 1:   Now Laurie – son – I've asked our club Chairman Mr Millichip to join us – to discuss the little matter you brought to me last week as he holds the purse strings so to speak.

81

ACTOR 3: That I do – and I keep a close grip on them I can tell you.

ACTOR 1: So perhaps we could start by you telling Mr Millichip why you're not happy with the new contract we're offering you for the next season.

ACTOR 3: And a very generous package it is too – especially for a young man of your – er – your – *(beat)* – how old are you?

ACTOR 2: Twenty three.

ACTOR 3: Even more generous than I thought then. I mean to say – how many other fellows like you are earning £120 a week.

ACTOR 1: What Mr Millichip is trying to say is we can't 'up' one player's wages without doing the same for all the others – and then where would we be – bankrupt – same as the country.

ACTOR 3: You can blame this bloody Labour Government for that!

ACTOR 1: The point is Laurie – son – we have to be fair –

ACTOR 3: Quite right – and there's no answer to that.

ACTOR 2: Not if it *was* fair – no – no – there'd be no answer at all.

ACTOR 3: What do you mean not fair?

ACTOR 2: Len Cantello, Bryan Robson, Ally Brown and Derek Statham are all on £200 quid a week – I get less than anyone else in the side and I'm the one who's just been picked for England – how that can be fair?

ACTOR 3: Yes – well – bugger fairness – it's moderation I'm on about.

ACTOR 2: And what about the contribution I made to the season?

ACTOR 3: What about it?

ACTOR 2: Beating Valencia in the UEFA Cup – top three finish in the First Division – was my contribution less than the other guys – you know – goals scored – goals laid on – crowds coming through the turnstiles to watch us play – money in the club's coffers – did I contribute any less than the others?

ACTOR 3: I'm not bankrupting this club just to keep you happy Cunningham.

ACTOR 2: All I'm asking for is £80 a week – so I'm on the same money as the other boys – I'm not asking for any more.

ACTOR 1: And I'm quite sure that this time next year we'll be able to review where we are now – all things being equal so to speak.

ACTOR 2: But they're not are they – they're nowhere near fucking equal!

ACTOR 1: No need for that sort of language son; we're all on the same side remember.

ACTOR 3:   And if you don't like you know what you can do.

ACTOR 1:   Not that we want to lose you son.

ACTOR 3:   And a bit of gratitude wouldn't go amiss.

ACTOR 2:   Gratitude?

ACTOR 3:   No bugger had ever heard of Laurie Cunningham when we signed you – and now here you are – playing in the top division with a top club – and that's down to us – and like I say you should be bloody grateful.

ACTOR 1:   The Chairman's does have a point Laurie –

ACTOR 3:   I bloody do.

ACTOR 1:   And you mark my words – this club has a great future – and you'll be part of that.

ACTOR 3:   So, come down off your high horse lad – 'cos a bit of humility wouldn't go amiss neither –

ACTOR 2:   Humility?

ACTOR 3:   That's the word I used – 'humility' – don't get too big for your boots 'cos you'll not find a better club than this.

ACTOR 2:   Is that so?

ACTOR 3:   I'm bloody sure of it.

ACTOR 2:   And what about Real Madrid?

ACTOR 3:   What about them?

ACTOR 2: They want to sign me.

ACTOR 1: Real Madrid?

ACTOR 2: Yes – they've been in touch.

ACTOR 3: Why haven't they gone through the proper channels?

ACTOR 2: They will do now.

ACTOR 1: What do you mean Laurie – 'they will do now'?

ACTOR 2: I said I didn't want to leave West Bromwich Albion – I told them I was happy here –

ACTOR 3: And so, you bloody well should be.

ACTOR 1: I'm glad you turned them down son – really glad.

ACTOR 2: I didn't.

ACTOR 1: I thought that's what you just said.

ACTOR 2: I asked them that if things were to change – if I stopped being happy – would they still be interested.

ACTOR 1: And?

ACTOR 2: All I've got to do is let them know and they'll make an official offer.

ACTOR 1: Yes – well – we can't have that – we can't have that can we Mr Chairman?

ACTOR 3: How much are they offering?

ACTOR 1: Hold on Mr Chairman – we don't want to lose Laurie – *(to Laurie)* – we don't want to lose you son.

ACTOR 2: You already have boss.

ACTOR 1: No – no – no – no – we can sort this out; we can sort this out can't we Mr Chairman –

ACTOR 3: Like I say – how much are they offering?

(The 3 Actors become street Newspaper sellers in both Britain and Spain)

ACTOR 1: *(shouting out as a street vendor)* Lea todo sobre esto – Laurie Cunningham firma para el Real Madrid –

ACTOR 2: *(shouting out as a street vendor)* Read all about it – Laurie Cunningham signs for Real Madrid –

ACTOR 3: *(shouting out as a street vendor)* Cunningham in million-pound transfer to the Bernabeu –

ACTOR 2: Cunningham en transferencia de un millón de libras al Bernabéu –

ACTOR 1: Cunningham – the first black player to sign for the World's Greatest Football Club!

ACTOR 3: El primer jugador negro en firmar para el mejor club de fútbol del mundo!

(The 3 Actors revert to become themselves)

ACTOR 1: And so we approach the apex –

ACTOR 2:   The zenith –

ACTOR 3:   The very pinnacle of his career –

ACTOR 1:   Real Madrid play away to the club they most
fear

(The 3 Actors sing the chorus to the song Barcelona in operatic style)

ALL: *(singing in operatic style)* Barcelona
It was the first time that we met
Barcelona
How can I forget
The moment that you stepped into the room
You took my breath away
Barcelona
La musica vibro
Barcelona
Yella nos unio
And if God is willing
We will meet again
Someday -

(The 3 Actors revert to become themselves)

ACTOR 2:   The Nou Camp Barcelona

ACTOR 1:   February 1980 – La Liga's crunch game –

ACTOR 3:   And a 100,000 Catalonians chant one name
alone–

(The 3 Actors become the Barcelona fans)

ACTORS 1 & 2: La Perla Negra! *(clap clap clap)*

ACTOR 3: 100,000 home fans stand in awe –

ACTOR 1: Not for their own side –

ACTOR 2: Not for a Barcelona star –

ACTOR 3: For the boy's skill – his grace – goes far beyond the partisan –

ACTORS 1 & 2: La Perla Negra! *(clap clap clap)*

ACTOR 3: Beyond the prejudice of the devoted fan –

ACTORS 1 & 2: La Perla Negra! *(clap clap clap)*

ACTOR 3: For here is a man imbued with that which surpasses enmity and the ancient feuds of division –

(The 3 Actors now become Laurie Cunningham and move in synchronised dance style to the actions they describe)

ACTOR 1: As those dazzling feet

Force full backs into retreat –

ACTOR 2: Leave them mesmerised –

ACTOR 1: Entranced –

ACTOR 3: As this Black Pearl glides –

ACTOR 2: Floats –

ACTOR 1: Dances his way goalwards –

(Beat)

ALL: Heavenwards.

(The 3 Actors now become mourners at Laurie Cunningham's graveside)

ACTOR 1: *(as the Priest)* God – into your hands we commend your son – Laurie –

ACTOR 2: *(direct to the audience)* Departed this life 15th July 1989 –

ACTOR 1: – in sure and certain hope –

ACTOR 3: *(direct to the audience)* Coruna Junction – Madrid – Spain –

ACTOR 1: *(as the Priest)* – certain hope of resurrection to eternal life through Jesus Christ our Lord – Amen. *(Beat)*

ACTOR 2: Aged 33 –

ACTOR 1: *(as the Priest)* Death, where is your sting? Grave, where is your victory?

(The 3 Actors revert to become themselves)

ACTOR 2: And whose victory shall it be?

ACTOR 3: What will be his legacy?

ACTOR 1: And who will have the final word?

(The 3 Actors become Enoch Powell and put on white face paint as they speak- The speech is intercut and juxtaposed with short recordings of voices saying what Laurie Cunningham meant to them)

ACTOR 1: *(as Enoch Powell)* We must be mad, literally mad –

ACTOR 2: *(as Enoch Powell)* It is like watching a nation busily engaged in heaping up its own funeral pyre.

ACTOR 3: *(as Enoch Powell)* While, to the immigrant, entry to this country was admission to privileges and opportunities eagerly sought –

ACTOR 1: *(as Enoch Powell)* – the impact upon the existing population was very different.

ACTOR 3: *(as Enoch Powell)* They found themselves made strangers in their own country.

RECORDING OF SPEECH 1:

Rhodene Cunningham:

I was only a young girl when he was taken so tragically on 15th July 1989 but the impact that he had on me and everyone close to him has never diminished. Although quietly spoken and gentle there was something magical in his nature that was deeply fascinating and people were instinctively drawn to him by his magnetic charisma. He was a man of super cool style and elegance who also wrote poetry, enjoyed painting and engaging in discussions on profound philosophical issues. He was also a brilliant freestyle dancer who combined the explosive energy of an athlete with the grace of ballet winning numerous competitions and cash prizes at the coolest clubs in town.

He was the magic dust of our lives that made us feel special and everything seem possible.

ACTOR 1: *(as Enoch Powell)* The other dangerous delusion… is summed up in the word "integration."

ACTOR 2: *(as Enoch Powell)* To be integrated into a population means to become for all practical purposes –

ALL: *(as Enoch Powell)* – indistinguishable from its other members.

RECORDING OF SPEECH 2:

Garth Crooks:

It wasn't just his blistering turn of pace that set him apart from the rest of the players but the way he seemed to glide past defenders, almost as though they weren't there. Laurie filled me with inspiration and although he didn't know it at the time was my role model. If he could play with such swaggering style and panache then why couldn't I? He brought an excitement, ingenuity, fashion and flair to a game that was often quite dull and predictable at times. More than that; he brought hope and inspiration to a whole generation of young black players.

ACTOR 3:   *(as Enoch Powell)* The discrimination and the deprivation, the sense of alarm and of resentment, lies not with the immigrant population –

ACTOR 2:   *(as Enoch Powell)* – but with those among whom they have come and are still coming.

RECORDING OF SPEECH 3:

David Lammy:

Laurie Cunningham's influence went way beyond football; he was a symbol of hope; he made black kids like me believe we could succeed in whatever field we chose.

ACTOR 1:   *(as Enoch Powell)* Here is the means of showing that the immigrant communities can organise to consolidate their members –

ACTOR 2:   *(as Enoch Powell)* – to agitate and campaign against their fellow citizens,

ACTOR 3:   *(as Enoch Powell)* and to overawe and dominate the rest. As I look ahead, I am filled with foreboding –

ALL: *(as Enoch Powell)* – like the Roman, I seem to see "the River Tiber foaming with much blood.

RECORDING OF SPEECH 4:

Nelson Mandela:

We hold it as an inviolable principle that racism must be opposed by all the means that humanity has at its disposal. Wherever it occurs it has the potential to result in a systematic and comprehensive denial of human rights to those who are discriminated against. This is because all racism is inherently a challenge to human rights, because it denies the view that every human being is a person of equal worth with any other, because it treats entire peoples as subhuman.

THE END